Published by b small publishing ltd.
www.bsmall.co.uk

Text and illustrations copyright © b small publishing ltd. 2022

1 2 3 4 5 ISBN 978-1-913918-23-1

Written, Designed and Illustrated by Kim Hankinson.
Editorial by Jenny Jacoby.

Printed in Malta by Gutenberg Press Ltd.

British Library Cataloguing-in-Publication Data.
A catalogue record for this book is available from the British Library.

We USE MATHS

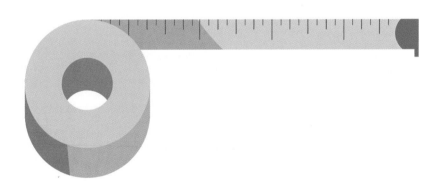

BY KIM HANKINSON

with STEM Editor

JENNY JACOBY

Meet the Everyday Maths Squad

COSTUME MAKER

PARK RANGER

PILOT

HOUSE BUILDER

PHOTOGRAPHER

CHEF

FOOTBALL COACH

House Builder

Building a house is like following a recipe! When we get to the building site, our foreman gives us jobs to do and we get to work as a team. The foreman works from plans (the recipe!), which are drawings that explain the design and sizes of everything.

We dig down before building up: first we lay **foundations**, then build the brick walls, and add a roof on top. Building sites can be busy and dangerous so we work in the safest way (and wear protective hard hats). We use maths to work out the best way to do each part of the job.

Certain shapes make a building strong ... and look nice too! Look around and see what **2D** shapes you can spot. Maybe the walls are rectangles or the roof might have a triangle at each end. If you look at enough buildings, you might see some more unusual shapes!

Another way geometry helps in building is the use of triangles, because they are the strongest shape. On the roof, we join wooden planks to create a triangle shape. If you press on the corner of a triangle shape it holds together. However, if you press on the corner of a square or rectangle, the sides push in to make a diamond or parallelogram. Knowing that triangles are strong is a great maths trick in construction!

We use geometry in our work, which is the study of shapes - every building is made up of shapes!

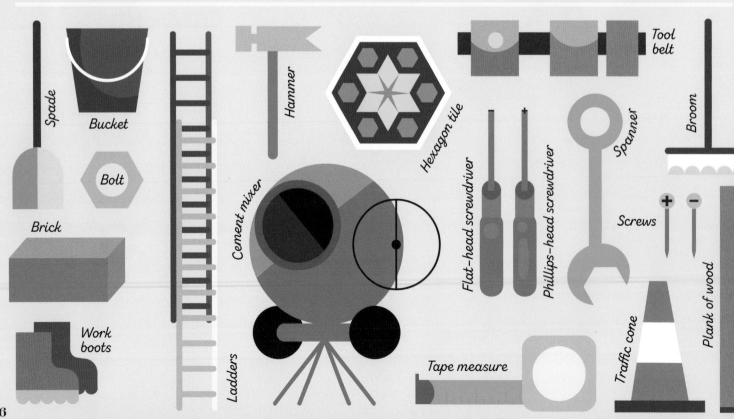

Spade

Bucket

Bolt

Brick

Work boots

Ladders

Hammer

Hexagon tile

Cement mixer

Tape measure

Flat-head screwdriver

Phillips-head screwdriver

Spanner

Screws

Traffic cone

Plank of wood

Broom

Tool belt

STRONG WALLS

A brick wall is made up of lots of rectangles, arranged so the ends of two bricks sit in the middle of the brick below. They fit together perfectly, which is called tessellation. The space between each brick is equal and filled with an even amount of cement. Building in a tessellating pattern means we don't waste any bricks and the wall is very neat and strong. Imagine if a brick wall were higgledy-piggledy – it wouldn't be as strong and you would have to use a lot more cement to hold it all together. It would also look weird!

TILE STYLE

Tiles protect walls and floors from water so they are often used to cover areas in a bathroom or kitchen that might get wet. Tiles fit perfectly without overlapping – that's another place where tessellation is used! You can see complex tessellations in amazing Arabic buildings, where tiles of different **interlocking** shapes and colours are arranged into beautiful geometric patterns. In fact, Arabic buildings are famous for their complex and beautiful **structures**, all created with maths in mind!

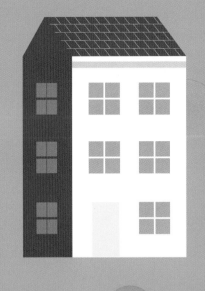

> Take a look at all the buildings around you and see if you can spot the mathematical shapes and patterns used to build them.

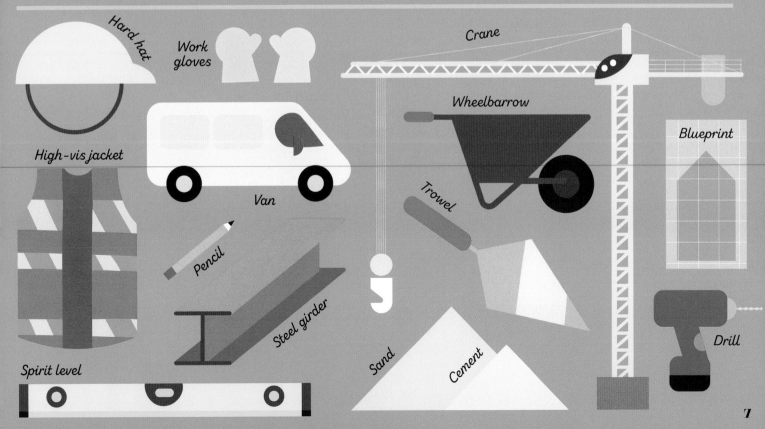

Hard hat

Work gloves

Crane

High-vis jacket

Wheelbarrow

Blueprint

Van

Pencil

Trowel

Steel girder

Drill

Spirit level

Sand

Cement

Costume Maker

Measure it, chalk it, cut it, pin it, sew it! We build outfits around the human body, twisting and joining 2D pieces of fabric into a **3D** costume!

Inspiration comes from everywhere – historical books, catwalk fashion, even nature ... whatever sparks our imagination. If everyone likes our sketches we then choose materials to make it from ... and figure out how to make it! Making clothes is a maths puzzle, and we need to create the pieces first.

Next step: we need some numbers. Tape measures flow and curl like a ribbon so we can **measure** you. Everyone is a different shape and no one has perfectly flat sides – if you did, you'd be shaped like a cardboard box! That's why we can't use a straight ruler.

Patterns are the blueprints for our designs and we draw them on paper to make sure the pieces and measurements match up. If we make a mistake it's easy to correct it on the pattern. We pin the cut-out paper pieces to huge rolls of fabric. We trace the design on to the fabric using chalk and cut out the flat shapes. We pin them together and sew them in place! Now we just add zips or buttons, and finishing touches ... remove all the pins ... and voila! You are the most wonderful dinosaur I ever saw!

We fashion theatrical creations using 3D geometry to make you look like a star!

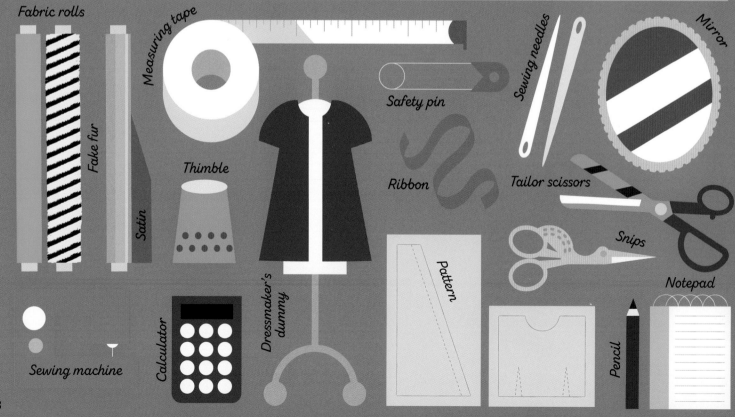

Fabric rolls

Fake fur

Satin

Measuring tape

Thimble

Dressmaker's dummy

Safety pin

Ribbon

Pattern

Sewing needles

Tailor scissors

Snips

Mirror

Notepad

Pencil

Sewing machine

Calculator

CREATING COSTUMES WITH MATHS

THE LINE OF SYMMETRY

Human bodies are pretty much **symmetrical** (but remember none of us is exactly the same on each side!) so we need our clothes to be symmetrical too. To make symmetry work, you need to know the line of symmetry. You can find it by standing alongside a mirror. This line shows us the two sides of a costume – each side needs to be a reflection of the other. Otherwise you'd have two left arms, not a right and left.

Rolling a piece of paper into a tube turns a 2D shape into a 3D one.

Finished costume

Line of symmetry

Left   Right

ALL THE WAY AROUND

Circumference

Beret

We loop the tape measure around your hips, waist and chest to measure you. The number where the end of the tape measure meets itself is the circumference. This word is used in maths to mean the length around any shape.

3D SHAPES

You can make a 2D sheet of paper into some of these 3D shapes. Have a play and see! Exploring creatively is great for learning, so don't worry if you don't get it right – it's all part of the process!

Ball   Pyramid   Cube   Cone   Cylinder

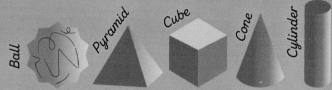

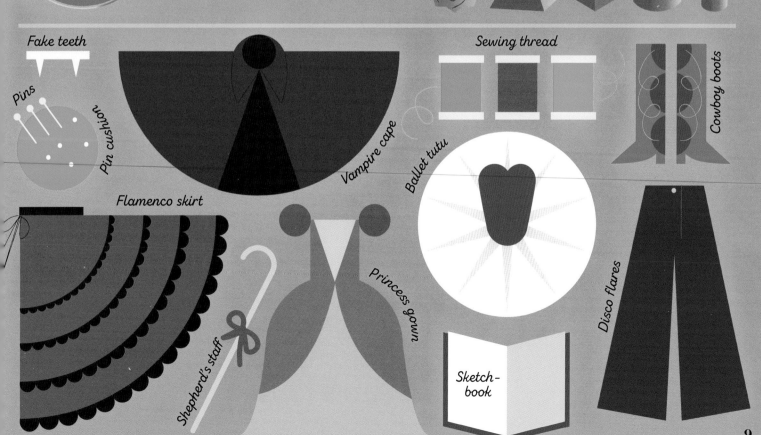

Fake teeth

Pins

Pin cushion

Flamenco skirt

Shepherd's staff

Vampire cape

Princess gown

Sketch-book

Sewing thread

Ballet tutu

Cowboy boots

Disco flares

Park Ranger

Welcome to the park! Protecting **endangered** birds in the forest, making safe a mountain trail, and keeping the lake clean for fish and visitors to swim in safely – that's what we park rangers do!

We use our **environmental** knowledge and some maths to protect all living things in the park, from big **mammals** such as deer, to tiny plants such as **lichen** on a tree trunk. We count them regularly and use the numbers to plan how to improve the park and keep it healthy. If an animal is seen less frequently each year, it might mean it needs somewhere safe to nest, or that its habitats are being damaged. Numbers show us what to investigate!

There's a lot of getting around to do too! In a wild **landscape** we use jeeps, bicycles, quad bikes, boats and our two feet – and ski sleds in snowy winters! How we travel depends on where we need to go. We might not want to disturb certain animals, and some places might not have tracks we can use. Maps help us work out how long it takes getting to different parts of the park, and how fast we can go. We use the same kind of maths to help visitors know just how long a hike will take before it gets dark.

Maps tell guests about the landscape in the park and help them plan their walk.

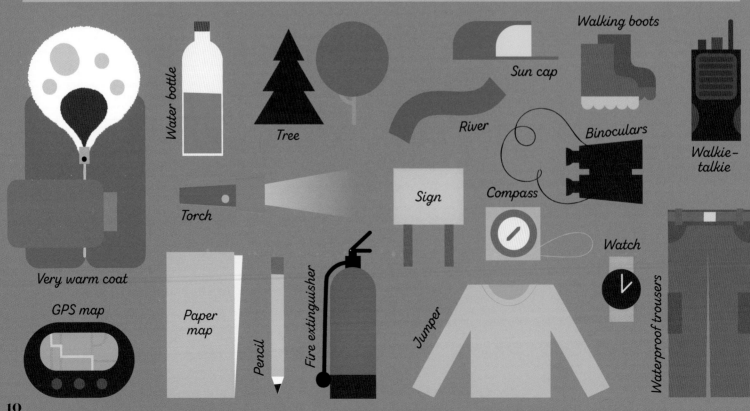

Very warm coat

GPS map

Water bottle

Torch

Paper map

Pencil

Fire extinguisher

Tree

River

Sign

Jumper

Sun cap

Compass

Binoculars

Watch

Walking boots

Walkie-talkie

Waterproof trousers

MAP MEASURE x MAP SCALE = REAL DISTANCE

Maps are a great tool for exploring the park as they are illustrated to scale. This means they are precisely a certain number of times bigger in the real world than in the map. Because of this you can plan your adventure using the tracks, paths and roads, understanding how far apart things really are. Maps also show key landmarks along the way, which help you work out where you are on the ground compared to the map – which is very handy when you're lost!

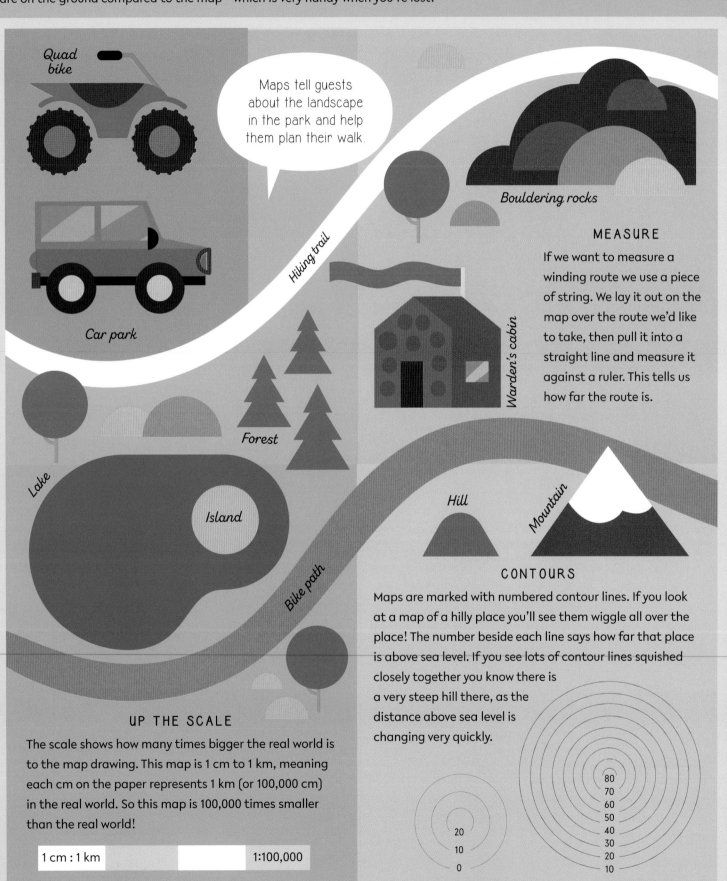

Quad bike

Maps tell guests about the landscape in the park and help them plan their walk.

Car park

Hiking trail

Bouldering rocks

Warden's cabin

Forest

Lake

Island

Hill

Mountain

Bike path

MEASURE

If we want to measure a winding route we use a piece of string. We lay it out on the map over the route we'd like to take, then pull it into a straight line and measure it against a ruler. This tells us how far the route is.

CONTOURS

Maps are marked with numbered contour lines. If you look at a map of a hilly place you'll see them wiggle all over the place! The number beside each line says how far that place is above sea level. If you see lots of contour lines squished closely together you know there is a very steep hill there, as the distance above sea level is changing very quickly.

UP THE SCALE

The scale shows how many times bigger the real world is to the map drawing. This map is 1 cm to 1 km, meaning each cm on the paper represents 1 km (or 100,000 cm) in the real world. So this map is 100,000 times smaller than the real world!

1 cm : 1 km   1:100,000

80
70
60
50
40
30
20
10

20
10
0

Shopkeeper

Welcome to the corner shop! Come in and you will see the prices of all the items we sell. All the foods have best before dates, which helps us make sure all the stock is fresh.

Sometimes we have special offers: buy one get one free, or half priced in a sale! It could get pretty complicated to work out the **discounts** but as we scan the **barcodes** the till does the maths for us and adds up the price of your shopping.

To pay, you can swipe or tap your bank card. The money whizzes straight from your bank account into the shop's! It's all done using computers. If you pay with cash, the register lets us know how much change to give you, then we make up your change from the coins and notes in the till.

When cash goes to the bank, they add it to our account. We don't get to keep everything! We need to pay for things like stock, staff, bags and repairs. When all of these costs are taken out, the money left over is noted in our accounts.

When we close the door at night, we put any cash in the safe, and put exactly the same amount of change in the till as we start with every day. Then we clean and restock our shelves ready to do it all over again!

There are lots of different numbers to look out for at your local shop!

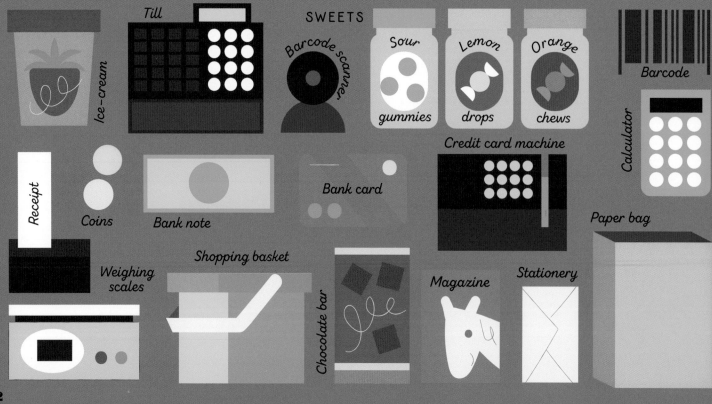

Ice-cream

Till

SWEETS

Barcode scanner

Sour gummies

Lemon drops

Orange chews

Barcode

Calculator

Credit card machine

Receipt

Coins

Bank note

Bank card

Paper bag

Weighing scales

Shopping basket

Chocolate bar

Magazine

Stationery

ONE PRICE

Anything with a barcode will have just one price but some of the things in the shop need to be measured.

2 kg

BANANAS £2 per kg

PRICE PER WEIGHT

Most of the fruit and vegetables have a different price per kilogram, so each type needs weighing separately. When we know the weight in kilograms, we find out the price by multiplying the weight by the price per kilogram.

1 (price per kg)   *2* (how many kg)   *2* (price in pounds)

3 (weight in kg)   *5* (weight in kg)   *3* (weight in kg)   *2* (weight in kg)

> Don't mix up different kinds of the same fruit or vegetables in your bag, as they often have different prices. No Granny Smith apples mingling with Pink Ladies, please!

HELPING THE ENVIRONMENT

At the filling station, small dry things like nuts, seeds and some liquids, are measured by weight too. Bring an empty jar from home and we can weigh it before you fill it. Then when you have filled it up I take away the weight of the empty jar from the total weight. This tells me the weight of the contents. Then I multiply the weight by the price per weight. This way you pay just for what's inside, and help save packaging!

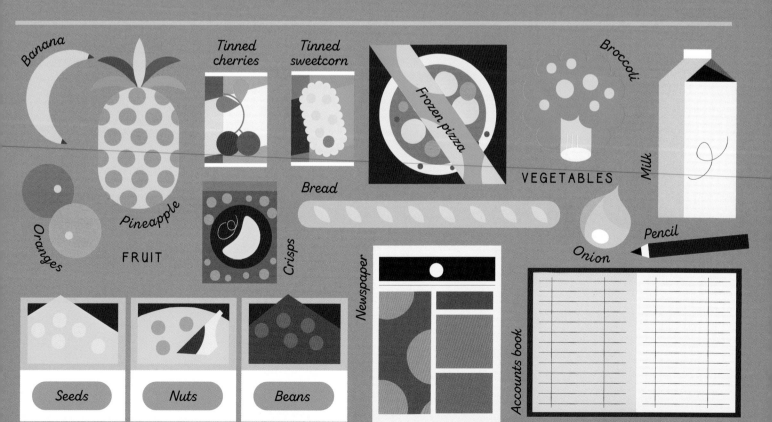

Banana · Tinned cherries · Tinned sweetcorn · Frozen pizza · Broccoli · Pineapple · FRUIT · Oranges · Bread · VEGETABLES · Milk · Crisps · Pencil · Onion · Newspaper · Accounts book · Seeds · Nuts · Beans

Weather Forecaster

The weather today will be mostly sunny with a chance of showers! And how do I know that? Well, we meteorologists (the fancy name for a weather forecaster) use maths to figure out what the weather is most likely to be.

Weather – from storms to sunshine – happens in our atmosphere. This is the huge blanket of air that surrounds our planet at about 200 km high. Meteorologists use lots of **equipment** to collect data about the atmosphere: satellite photography to see clouds, radar towers to map where rain is falling, and weather stations in remote places such as Mount Everest, Antarctica, ocean ships and aeroplanes.

To predict local weather, first we look out of the window! The height and shape of clouds show us things. A tall cumulonimbus means a storm!

Local weather stations record everything else we need: temperature, wind speed, wind direction and **air pressure**. Air pressure is the weight of the atmosphere around us – it changes because the sun warms the air differently in different places. When air is warm it moves about, spreading then **compressing** then spreading out again. When the wind suddenly picks up it's more than likely because the air is moving as the pressure changes!

We compare the data to patterns of weather from the past, using maps, charts and simulations so we can tell what is most likely to happen next.

We use maths to help us forecast tomorrow's weather!

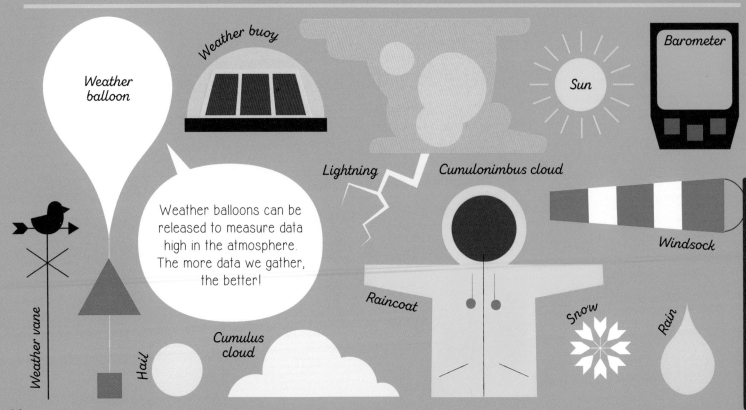

Weather balloon

Weather buoy

Barometer

Sun

Weather balloons can be released to measure data high in the atmosphere. The more data we gather, the better!

Lightning

Cumulonimbus cloud

Windsock

Raincoat

Weather vane

Hail

Cumulus cloud

Snow

Rain

TURNING NUMBERS INTO WEATHER PREDICTIONS

Numbers are a really important part of the forecasting puzzle! A weather station collects lots of information, which we then put into something called a mathematical model. This is a set of **equations** we have worked out by looking at the way the weather usually works. The weather is controlled by natural laws and so changes in weather are not random. When we put numbers into these equations, the models predict what will happen next. It's magical maths at its most mind-blowing!

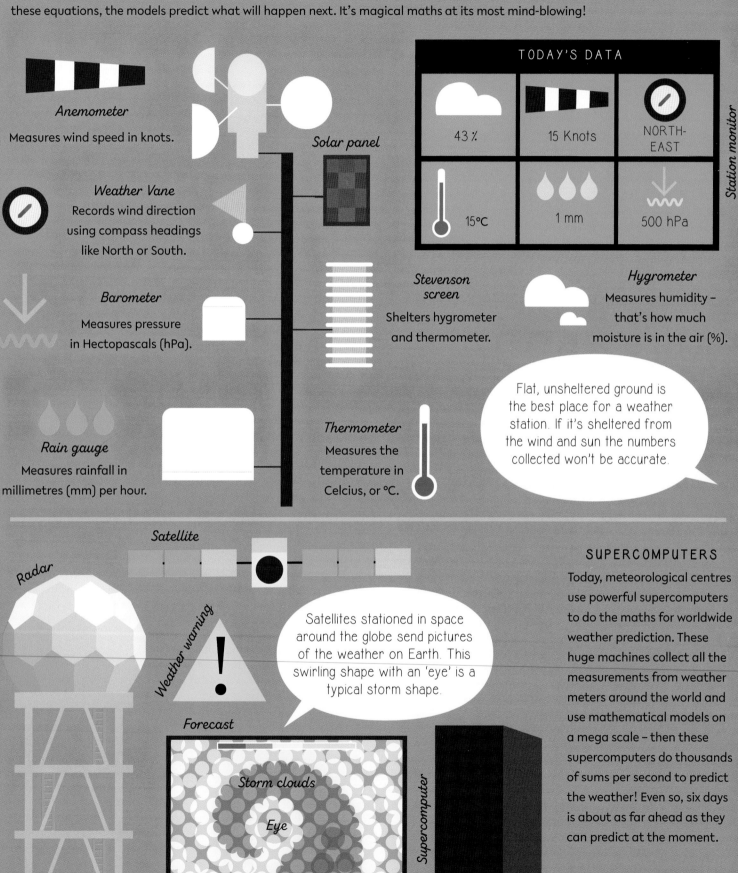

Anemometer
Measures wind speed in knots.

Solar panel

Weather Vane
Records wind direction using compass headings like North or South.

Barometer
Measures pressure in Hectopascals (hPa).

Stevenson screen
Shelters hygrometer and thermometer.

Hygrometer
Measures humidity – that's how much moisture is in the air (%).

Rain gauge
Measures rainfall in millimetres (mm) per hour.

Thermometer
Measures the temperature in Celcius, or °C.

TODAY'S DATA

43 %	15 Knots	NORTH-EAST
15°C	1 mm	500 hPa

Station monitor

Flat, unsheltered ground is the best place for a weather station. If it's sheltered from the wind and sun the numbers collected won't be accurate.

Satellite

Radar

Weather warning

!

Satellites stationed in space around the globe send pictures of the weather on Earth. This swirling shape with an 'eye' is a typical storm shape.

Forecast

Storm clouds

Eye

Supercomputer

SUPERCOMPUTERS

Today, meteorological centres use powerful supercomputers to do the maths for worldwide weather prediction. These huge machines collect all the measurements from weather meters around the world and use mathematical models on a mega scale – then these supercomputers do thousands of sums per second to predict the weather! Even so, six days is about as far ahead as they can predict at the moment.

Pilot

Welcome aboard this flight! Buckle up as you take your seat. I am your captain of this A380 plane – the largest passenger aircraft in the world! The co-pilot and I are performing our pre-flight checks in the **cockpit** at the front, before we taxi you to the runway for take-off. We check our dials and switches connected to the plane's computer to make sure everything is just right for a safe and pleasant journey.

It can be very exciting flying to different towns and cities. Travelling by air allows us to move at super high speeds of just under 1,000 kph. There is even a direct flight from one side of the globe to the other: London, England to Perth, Australia takes around 17 hours. That sounds long but in the sky there are very few obstacles, so our flights can go fast safely.

As a pilot I need to be good at solving problems and able to do lots of calculations quickly and correctly. We use geometry to map out the routes of flight paths, and have to understand the best angles for safe take-offs and landings. We make sure we have enough runway to slow down on, and can safely land at the right angle and speed. Touchdown!

We need to understand a lot of measurements in our job! Maths keeps planes flying safely!

Runway

27

Pilot's licence

Uniform

Headphones

Microphone

Pilot's logbook

Flight plan

Aviator shades

Sunscreen

FACTOR 50

Pencil

Snack

YUM BAR

Torch

Window visor

Drink

Cockpit

We monitor different speeds during a flight: true airspeed, wind speed and ground speed. We measure in units called knots. Planes fly because of their **aerodynamic** shape, the conditions in the sky and the power of the plane. Planes can move to higher or lower altitudes (distance from the ground) by changing speed.

TRUE AIRSPEED

The airspeed indicator tells pilots how fast the plane is moving compared to the air around it. It is calculated by onboard computers using a speed gauge and other data about the air conditions around the plane. Things like altitude and weather change the true airspeed, so the computer uses some pretty clever maths!

WIND SPEED

This is the speed of the wind around the plane. A headwind pushes against the front of the plane and slows it down, but a tailwind pushes at the back and makes it a little faster. Tailwinds created by storms over the Atlantic Ocean have made flights from New York to London almost two hours quicker!

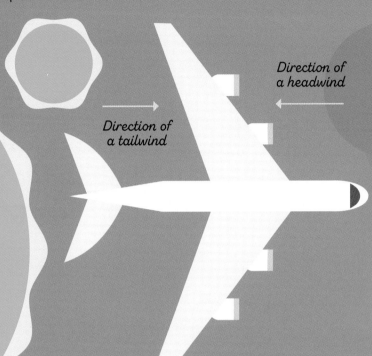

Direction of a headwind

Direction of a tailwind

We use airspeed and the length of the flight path to calculate how much time the flight will take.

GROUND SPEED

This is how fast the aircraft would be flying if it were on the ground. It is worked out using the wind speed and airspeed, but we also use GPS in newer planes. The air really high up is different to the air lower down, meaning we fly at great ground speeds when we are high up in the air!

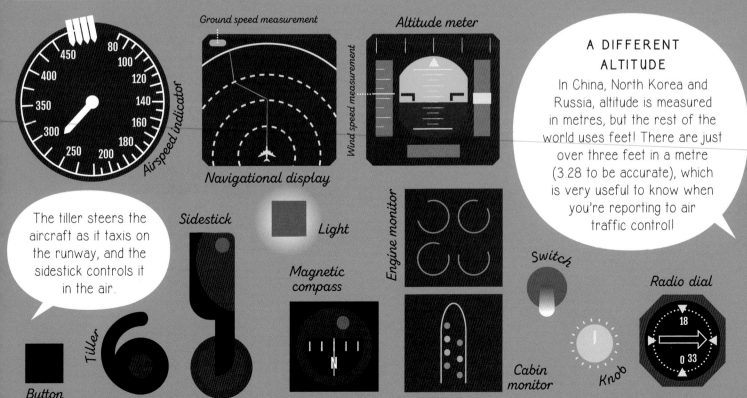

Ground speed measurement

Altitude meter

Wind speed measurement

Airspeed indicator

Navigational display

A DIFFERENT ALTITUDE

In China, North Korea and Russia, altitude is measured in metres, but the rest of the world uses feet! There are just over three feet in a metre (3.28 to be accurate), which is very useful to know when you're reporting to air traffic control!

The tiller steers the aircraft as it taxis on the runway, and the sidestick controls it in the air.

Sidestick

Light

Magnetic compass

Engine monitor

Switch

Radio dial

Tiller

Cabin monitor

Knob

Button

Vet

Animals show us they're ill by behaving in an unusual way. The pet's owner can tell us the most about what's wrong because they know the pet's normal character and habits. We also use tools and record numbers to work out what might be wrong. Changes in their weight or heart rate when compared to records taken on a previous visit can tell us a lot!

X-rays are a great way to see what's going on inside the pet. The machine sends X-rays all the way through the body and then on to a film on the other side. As X-rays hit the film, it turns black. Things like bones (or perhaps a chewy toy your dog shouldn't have eaten) block some or all of the X-rays, and where those rays don't reach the film it stays white – that's how the picture ends up black and white! Only one more thing to do now for the perfect picture: hold very still!

Sometimes animals will need medicine to get better and each animal needs different amounts of medicine. There is a lot to think about!

Maths helps us understand what an animal needs, without being able to talk to them.

Gloves

Cone

Vivarium

Jim the lizard

Mask

Tablets

Scrubs

Scissors

Bowl

Daisy the dog

Stethoscope

Moon the cat

Goldfish

Charlie the cockatiel

Syringe

Microscope

Otoscope

Perch

Razor

Terry tarantula

Bandage

Medicine

WHY WE WEIGH PETS

As a vet we need to make sure we give your pet the right amount of medicine. Too much medicine in the body is never good, so we use some clever maths to get this right!

First, we weigh your pet, because we know how much medicine to give each animal based on its weight. The heavier an animal the more medicine its body will need. Very light animals need less medicine.

The scales show us that number in kilograms. One kilogram is about the weight of a pineapple. If your pet weighs 3 kg, she weighs about the same as three pineapples!

By knowing the right kind of medicines to give each kind of animal, and their weight, we give the animal just the right dose of medicine to make them better!

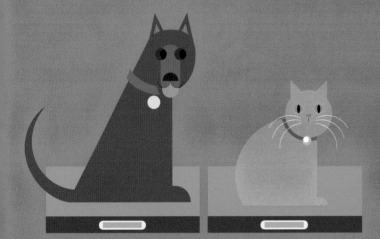

MIXED-UP MEDICINES

There is one more number we need before giving medicine to a pet. We look at the percentage on the label – this tells us how strong the medicine is inside. Medicines made of the same ingredients can be made up into different strengths.

It's is a bit like how much squash you put into a glass, and how much water you add. If you only use a little squash and a lot of water, you have a low **percentage** of squash. If you do half and half you'd have 50 percent squash and 50 percent water ... and a VERY sweet drink, eurgh!

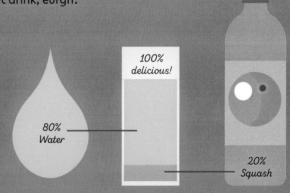

80% Water

100% delicious!

20% Squash

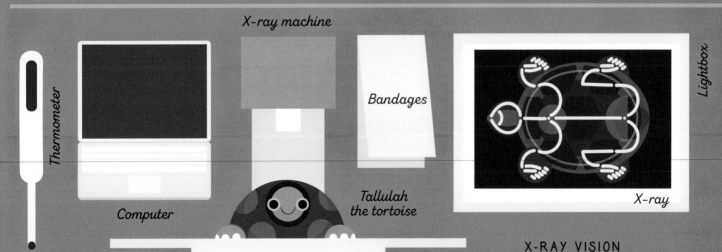

Thermometer

X-ray machine

Bandages

Lightbox

Computer

Tallulah the tortoise

X-ray

X-ray table

Weighing scales

Whitney the mouse

X-RAY VISION

X-rays are pretty cool and let us see what's going on inside. Strong X-rays can be bad for us and our pets too, so we want to use the lowest power we can to get a good X-ray picture. We use maths to calculate the right amount of tube **current** and **voltage** for an animal's size and shape. This gives a clear image without causing harm.

Photographer

Can you think what a mountain top looks like? What about a wild animal or the Eiffel tower? Chances are that even if you've never seen these things in person you know what they look like from seeing a photograph, taken by a camera.

A camera works by recording light travelling through a lens on to a film or **sensor**. Though digital cameras record images on a memory card and film cameras on to film, both cameras work in much the same way.

Every camera has a shutter just in front of where the film or digital sensor sits. The shutter usually stays closed so light can't get inside. But when you press the button to take a picture, the shutter quickly opens and closes, letting in light for a short burst. This is how a photo is taken. You can adjust how fast the shutter opens and closes, which changes what a photo will look like.

We can also choose between lots of different lenses. Zoom lenses allow the camera to see way into the distance. This is especially handy for wildlife photographers who don't want to be noticed! **Macro** lenses allow you to get super close-up pictures of small things. We can also play with how dark the image is and how much of it is in **focus**. You can get really creative with the pictures you take!

> We need an artistic eye and maths skills to make the camera settings work together and take a great photo!

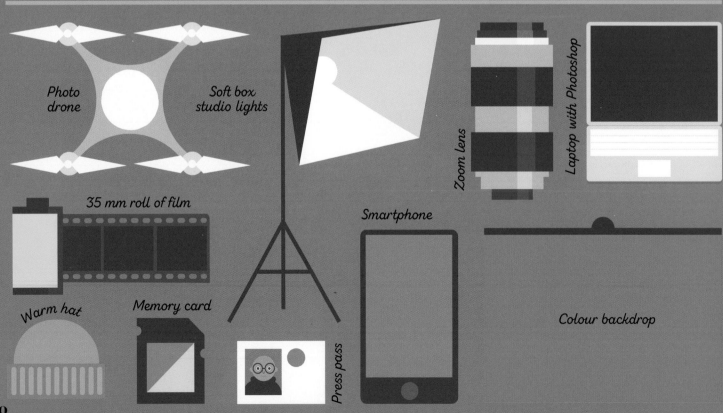

Photo drone

Soft box studio lights

Zoom lens

Laptop with Photoshop

35 mm roll of film

Smartphone

Warm hat

Memory card

Press pass

Colour backdrop

SHUTTER SPEED

Fast shutter speeds are good for capturing a precise moment. This is great for anything that's moving … and not many things stay perfectly still! Some special cameras have shutter speeds so fast they can take a crisp picture of a hummingbird's wings in flight! Slow shutter speeds help you capture a longer moment in one image. While the shutter is open, the camera layers each moment on to one still image. This can make moving car lights look like strings! The camera needs to stay perfectly still while the shutter is open, so we use a tripod to keep it steady – otherwise you'd record the movement of the camera too.

Shutter button *Flash* *Lens*

FOCAL LENGTH

If you look on the side of an **SLR camera** lens, you'll see numbers measuring how far the lens inside is from the sensor (or film). Playing with this length changes how much of the photograph will be detailed and clear.

APERTURE

The aperture is the opening inside the camera, and playing with the 'f-stop' setting changes its size, allowing more or less light into the camera when the shutter is open. The bigger the aperture, the more of the picture that will be in focus – but that will also make the image look flatter. If there is only a small area in focus and the rest blurred, the image will look like it has lots of depth!

BALANCING LIGHT

Because both aperture and shutter speed affect the amount of light let inside the lens, we need to make these numbers work together. We use maths to balance the light we let in. A low f-stop lets more light in, so we need to balance that with a fast shutter speed … otherwise, too much light will make the picture **overexposed** – maybe even totally white! A high f-stop and fast shutter speed might mean not enough light gets in, and you can end up with a totally black image instead.

> Light meters measure the light where we are shooting and show us which shutter speed and f-stop to use. We can use lights and reflectors to help us get different effects.

Computer back-up

Lens cap

Light meter

Umbrella light

Notepad

Flash

Pencil

Tripod

Backpack

Light reflector

Filters

Viewfinder

Digital camera

Football Coach

When I blow my whistle it's go time! Coaches select and train sportspeople to be the best they can. We train really hard, make our players eat and sleep well and create game **tactics** and **strategies**.

In a fast game like football things don't always go as planned! Instead of pretending they will, we try to increase the chance of getting things right. Using **statistics** and **probability**, we try to select the right team for each match and pick the best strategy to win.

By choosing the best player for each position, you increase your chance of winning. A brilliant goal scorer is best playing as a forward. This position is closest to the opponent's goal, so it has the most opportunities to score.

World-class sports teams everywhere have researchers who use maths to collect huge amounts of information from matches and games. They create **computer models** that show the coach how to build the right team for each game. Liverpool United signed up superscorer Mohamed Salah and coach Jürgen Klopp based on what their models suggested! With these two at the club, Liverpool United won the UK Premier League, the European Championship AND the FIFA World Cup. Now, that's some smart maths!

We use statistics to help us choose our teams and strategise for matches.

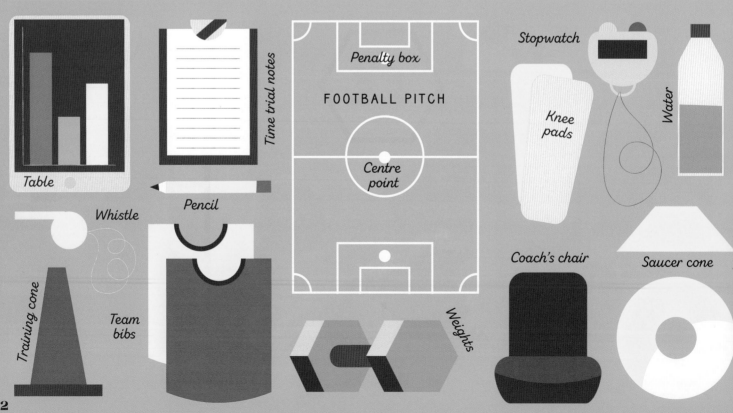

Table

Time trial notes

Penalty box

FOOTBALL PITCH

Centre point

Stopwatch

Knee pads

Water

Whistle

Pencil

Training cone

Team bibs

Weights

Coach's chair

Saucer cone

DATA COLLECTION

Collecting numbers is the first step in statistics. We look at the numbers (called 'data') in detail and decide what it means, but first we need to make sure we get lots of accurate data. We record specific information during practice and matches to help us know each player's strengths and weaknesses. We might time how fast each team member runs a circuit, or note down the number of times a player wins a tackle. Putting the data into visual **tables**, **graphs** and **charts** helps us see the information we have recorded and what it means. It is much easier to understand data as a picture than a big pile of numbers! Data makes it easy to plan strategies.

A tiny difference in the angle the ball hits the goal post can be the difference between it bouncing off or going in and scoring a goal. There are a lot more numbers in sports than the final score!

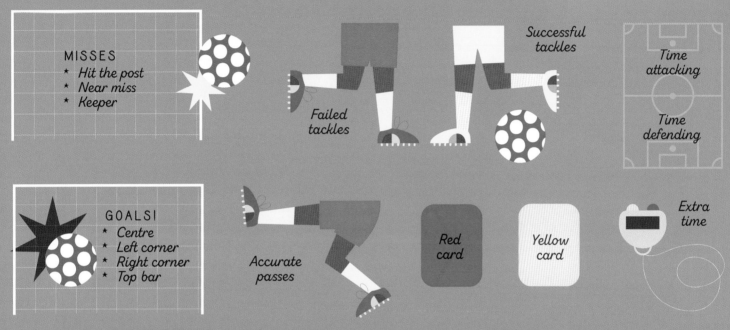

MISSES
★ Hit the post
★ Near miss
★ Keeper

Failed tackles

Successful tackles

Time attacking

Time defending

GOALS!
★ Centre
★ Left corner
★ Right corner
★ Top bar

Accurate passes

Red card

Yellow card

Extra time

Have a go at collecting data for a sport you enjoy next time you're watching a match or game. These are for football, but you can make up your own for any sport. See what you can find out!

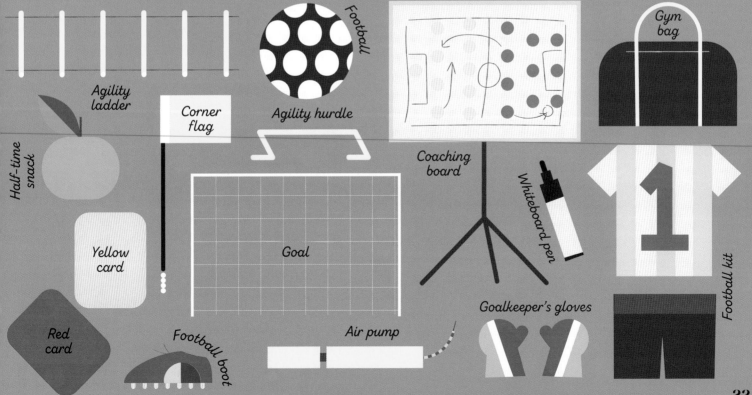

Agility ladder

Corner flag

Football

Agility hurdle

Coaching board

Gym bag

Half-time snack

Yellow card

Goal

Whiteboard pen

Red card

Football boot

Air pump

Goalkeeper's gloves

Football kit

DJ

Pop, alternative, jazz, disco, electronic dance music ... listen carefully to any song, and you will hear that it is not a random string of noises. Songs are made up of patterns of sounds repeating. These patterns are actually mathematical! Weirdly, what sounds good to our human ears actually follows maths rules too – though we don't need to understand it to enjoy music!

The patterns the piece of music follows can tell us what style it is. Motown often contains some horns, trumpets, an organ, and singing in **harmony**. Reggae has many of the same instruments but the way they are played is really different – and a big part of the difference in sound is the patterns of the **rhythm** and **beat**!

When I am playing a dance set, I can make one tune flow into the next as the bpm (beats per minute) is similar for songs in that music style. The audience can only hear the music coming from the speakers, but I can hear the next record on my headphones (that's why I only cover one ear with the headphones – so I can hear both tunes at the same time). If I want to blend the two tunes, I adjust the position and speed of the next song to line up the beat, and when they are in time, I swap the volumes so the old track fades out as the other one starts coming in through the speakers! It's a bit like patting your head and rubbing your tummy in time. Give it a go ... perhaps you are a natural DJ!

We use maths to make sure you enjoy listening to the songs we choose to play!

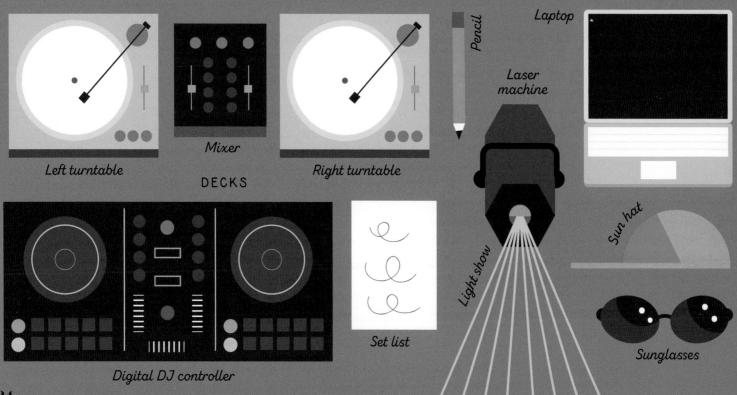

Left turntable

Mixer

DECKS

Right turntable

Pencil

Laptop

Laser machine

Light show

Sun hat

Digital DJ controller

Set list

Sunglasses

FEEL THE BEAT

The speed (known as 'tempo') of music beats, and the patterns in which they are played (the rhythm) have a big impact on what we hear. High bpm makes us feel energised: can you think of a song that makes you want to jump up and down? Is it fast or slow? Researchers have found that feel-good pop songs have a tempo of about 150 bpm, which is pretty fast. There aren't always sounds on every single beat – it's a silent count that keeps time. The bpm of hip–hop music is around 80 – 115, whereas electronic dance music (EDM) is around 128 bpm. As lining up the beats is key to DJing, it's important to know about tempo!

See if you can count the tempo and pat along with the rhythm of your favourite songs ... it's pretty tricky!

SET THE TEMPO

Using a timer, you are going to set a tempo by clapping once every second. There are 60 seconds in a minute so you will clap 60 times in one minute at this pace. You've just set a tempo of 60 bpm.

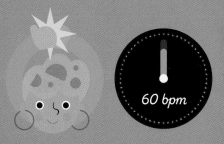

60 bpm

Now, try clapping every other second. You will be clapping at 30 bpm, half the number of beats!

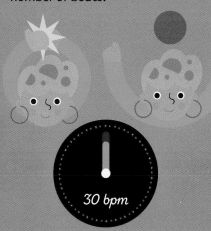

30 bpm

When we hear patterns in music our brains are understanding some pretty complex maths without us really even noticing!

RHYTHM

Rhythm is played to the tempo's beat. Rhythm is the beats we can hear and the pattern they make. Rhythm beats can be loud or soft and long or short. Rhythms can be complicated, but they follow the same simple maths. To set a rhythm, clap your hands on the first beat and then pat your chest for the next 3.

Repeat. This rhythm is 4 beats long.

Create different rhythms of different lengths to your bpm tempos!

Record

Compact disc

Headphones

Speakers

Music collection

Cool clothes

Smoke

Water bottle

Fancy dress

Microphone

Record bag

Smoke machine

Interior Designer

Right, let's look at this space, and see what we can do to restyle it. First, I take photos and make a drawing of the room from above, which is called a plan. I jot down the measurements of the room so I can understand the shape and size of the room accurately.

Next is colour! Do you have a favourite colour? This is something I always ask the person I'm designing the room for as it's important they like it! We can use lots of one colour and then add little bits of other colours, called accents. Or we could use one colour in various shades ... that's how light or dark, or strong or soft it might be. There is a rainbow of colours to choose from so I need to be careful to choose ones that look good together.

Next comes the mood board. I bring together a collection of fabric **swatches** and pictures for inspiration. Sometimes the design is inspired by a particular style with its own rules. Art deco, for example, is made up of straight, sharp lines, whereas rococo style features curling **floral** details. You can tell one style from another because the colours, shapes and textures follow certain patterns and sometimes even mathematical rules.

Then it's time to sketch my ideas. If my client likes my designs, we get to work on the real thing. Then the adventure really begins!

We combine art and mathematics to make beautiful designs.

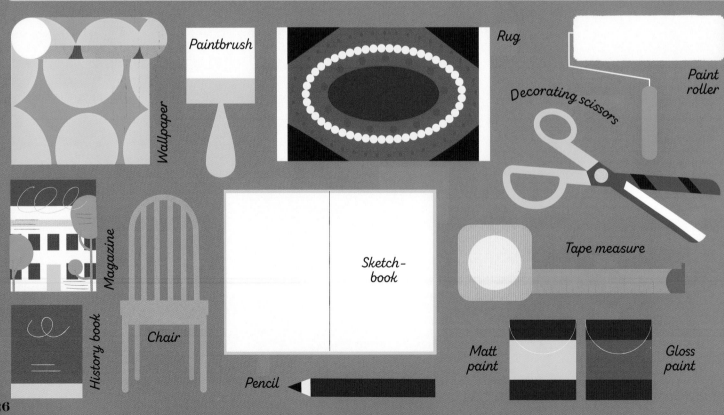

Wallpaper

Paintbrush

Rug

Decorating scissors

Paint roller

Magazine

Sketch-book

Tape measure

History book

Chair

Pencil

Matt paint

Gloss paint

PERSPECTIVE: DRAWING WITH MATHS

To get a better idea of how the final room will look I make a drawing using a one-point **perspective** guide to make the picture more realistic. It's a mathematical method that was used by great painters hundreds of years ago to give a picture depth, and was an important art discovery. Before then everything had looked very flat indeed!

MOOD BOARD

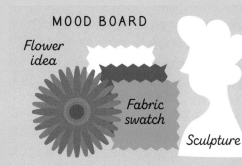

Flower idea

Fabric swatch

Sculpture

Vase

Photo

Sea theme

Curtain

Column

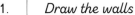

1. *Draw the walls*

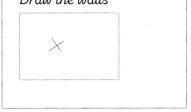

A big rectangle is the closest edge of the room. The smaller one inside is the far wall. Draw a point inside the smaller one with an X.

2. *Add ceiling & floor*

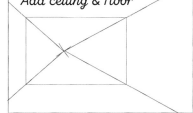

Draw 4 lines starting at your X and going straight through each corner of the smaller box. Rub out the lines from the smaller box.

3. *Add wall details*

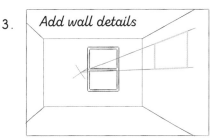

Draw in any details on the back wall as flat shapes. For the left or right wall start from the X to get the shape right.

4. *Add furniture*

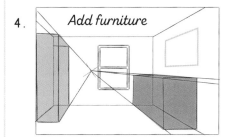

For a 3D shape, start with a rectangle for the closest edge then draw lines from the X through the corners of the rectangle. Use these guides to draw a smaller rectangle behind and complete the shapes.

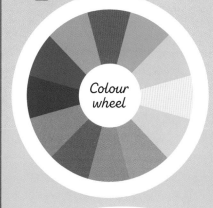

Colour wheel

Colour wheels tell us which colours will look good together. First, select one colour, then choose the one on the opposite side of the wheel as they will complement each other!

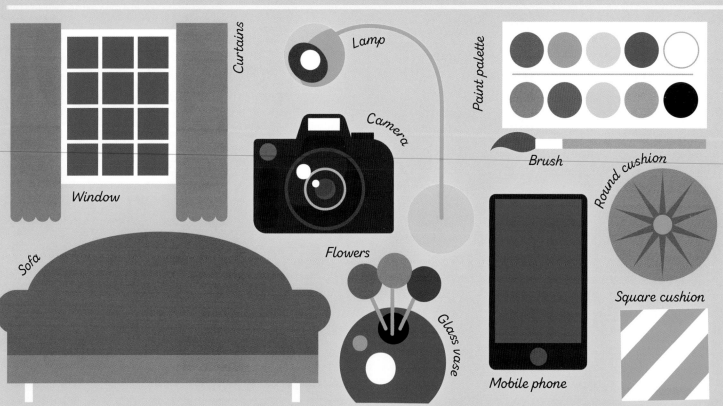

Curtains

Window

Lamp

Camera

Paint palette

Brush

Flowers

Glass vase

Mobile phone

Round cushion

Square cushion

Sofa

Chef

Let's get those orders up and out! There is a lot of noise flying around in a hotel kitchen – we chefs are used to the noise and heat as we steam, boil, **sauté**, roast and fry!

Chefs like me follow recipes from the head chef. In a kitchen we work our way up, taking time to learn each skill as we go. Time is a huge part of all cooking and we take it very seriously in a kitchen! We learn to chop at high speed so we can prepare the huge mountain of food ready for each sitting. We keep track of how long customers have waited, and make the dishes so all the food for one table leaves the kitchen together, even though each person might have ordered different things that take different times to cook. We can't leave it waiting for too long or it will get cold.

Making food is kitchen **chemistry** and cooking time is one of the ingredients you can change to get different results. Trying to do things too quickly could give you custard that looks like scrambled eggs, or cakes with a burnt, bitter outside and a runny middle – no one wants to eat that! We want to see empty plates and happy customers, please. Yes, chef!!

We use equations to work out the perfect cooking time and temperature for our delicious recipes.

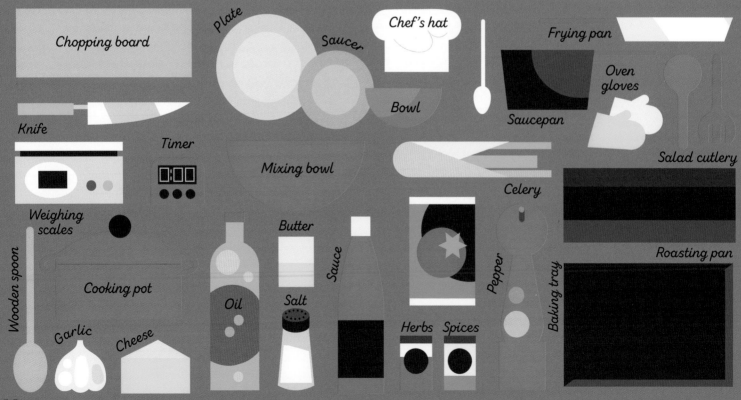

Chopping board

Plate

Saucer

Chef's hat

Frying pan

Oven gloves

Bowl

Saucepan

Salad cutlery

Knife

Timer

Mixing bowl

Celery

Weighing scales

Butter

Sauce

Pepper

Roasting pan

Baking tray

Wooden spoon

Cooking pot

Oil

Salt

Herbs   Spices

Garlic

Cheese

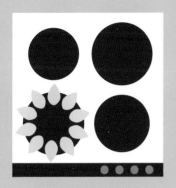

STEAK

With a little oil in the pan, food touching a hot metal frying pan will cook super fast. It's a pretty intense way to cook! Food needs to be thin and flat to cook this way. You need to turn it over to cook each side, and the heat needs to get inside and cook the middle before the outside burns. The equation for cooking steak is ...

5 minutes + 5 minutes

= 10 minutes

ROAST CHICKEN

An oven bakes or roasts food. Surrounding the food with hot air cooks it on all sides at once. It's less hot than a frying pan so food takes longer to cook, but we can adjust the time and make sure it has enough time to cook all the way through. When we roast a ginormous pumpkin or a turkey, heat needs a lot of time to cook it in the middle. There are perfect temperatures to do this and special formulas to get it just right.

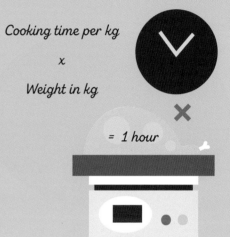

Cooking time per kg

x

Weight in kg

= 1 hour

PIZZA

Pizza ovens combine both hot air and intense heat from below. When you pop a pizza straight into the bottom of the pizza oven, it cooks the base super fast to make it crispy, while hot air in the bell-shaped oven circulates around the top, melting the delicious cheese. A plain pizza needs just two minutes to cook to perfection!

Pizza cooking time = 2 minutes

ORDERS UP!

If you order pizza, your brother roast chicken and your mum a steak, we need to make sure all the dishes are hot and ready at the same time. We plan this well before you even come into the restaurant as otherwise you'd have to wait at least an hour for your food!

1 HOUR

We started cooking the chicken an hour before you came in so it is ready to eat. We can keep it warm.

10 MINUTES

Steak needs to be cooked to order. This dish takes the most time to prepare from your order. We time everything else around this dish!

2 MINUTES

Pizza needs to be cooked fresh but in just 2 minutes. We cook it 8 minutes after the steak begins cooking.

Glossary

Here are some words from the book that you might not know!

2D – a flat shape like a square

3D – a shape that has depth such as a cube

Aerodynamic – can move through the air easily

Air pressure – the weight of the air above us

Barcodes – data in a pattern that a machine can read

Beat – a way of measuring musical time

Chart – a collection of information

Chemistry – the science of what everything is made of

Cockpit – the part of the plane where the pilot sits

Compressing – squashing something to make it smaller

Computer model – an example of what might happen

Current – the flow of electricity

Discounts – money taken off the full price of a product

Endangered – at risk of becoming extinct

Environmental – to do with the health of the world around us

Equations – sums that help you find missing information

Equipment – special tools

Floral – to do with flowers

Focus – how clearly you can see something

Foundations – the base of a building that holds the rest up

Graphs – a visual way to show how information is related

Harmony – sounds that are nice when heard together

Interlocking – when two or more separate things are connected securely

Landscapes – an area of land made up of different features

Lichen – a crusty plant that grows on the side of a tree

Macro – to do with the bigger picture and the wider world

Mammals – warm-blooded animals with live young

Measure – find out the size or weight of something

Overexposed – too much light hit the lens, spoiling a photo

Percentage – how many times something goes into 100

Perspective – the angle from which you look at something

Probability – how likely something is to happen

Rhythm – a repeated pattern of sounds in music

Sauté – to fry something

Sensor – machine that senses what is around it

SLR camera – a 'single-lens reflex' camera that gives the photographer an accurate view

Statistics – collecting numbers and looking for information

Strategies – clever ways of planning for a result

Structures – a building or an idea made up of different parts

Swatches – examples of colour or how materials will look

Symmetrical – when something is the same on both sides

Tables – a grid of numbers

Tactics – tricks that help you

Voltage – how high or low the amount of electricity is

#MathsSquad

Dedicate a whole day to maths. On that day, try and look for these key mathematical concepts all around you.

Now you have discovered that maths is everywhere, here are some ways you can become part of the maths squad too.

Calculations

Angles

Counting

Data

Measurements

Money

Statistics

Shapes

Make a #MathsSquad notebook out of scrap paper and write down or draw what you find. Rank your discoveries in order from most surprising to least surprising. Where was the most unexpected place or time that you came across maths in your day?

Question Time

Interview an adult or grown-up friend of the family about the everyday tasks they do in their job or at home. Take some notes in your #MathsSquad notebook and compare against the everyday maths above. Can you find some unexpected maths in their day? You might surprise even them!